PINK & HOT PINK HABITAT

PINK & HOT PINK HABITAT

Natalie Lyalin

Coconut Books
Atlanta, GA
2009

Copyright © 2009 by Natalie Lyalin
Published by Coconut Books
www.coconutpoetry.org
All rights reserved
ISBN: 978-0-578-02584-1
Cover Design: Shanna Compton
Cover Image: Matt Cipov
Interior Layout: Jon Link

For my grandmother, Galina Slonim Kravets
Моей бабушке Галине Слоним-Кравец посвящается

Contents

1.

Opalescent 11
Goose Necks for the Baby Baby 12
The Miniature Life of a Raven 13
Boy Birds 14
Calf's Blood 15
Technical / Vocational 16
Watch the Village .17
Dangerfields 18
Many Teens Hide Deepest Secrets in Plain Sight 19
Pink and Hot Pink Habitat 20
Breasts of America 21
Düsseldorf is For Sisters 22
Autumn. Sugar. Bloodspring.. 23
Misarubka 24

2.

Super Dolphin (Super Skin) 27
Me in Prison 28
Maybe Someone is Altering Your Throat 29
From the Suitcase My Back is an Arrow 30
Buffalo Cuffs 31
Weakened Astronauts 32
New Jersey Seems Magical 33
No One is Brunswick Turbulon 34
Miss Sarajevo 35
Mathematic Horse 36
The Cloisters 37

Great Sophias. 38
The Decorating Committee 39
A) Geography 40
Jeffrey Bloodhound Sans 41

3.

All Night Vigil 45

4.

Von Furstenberg 55
There Are Four Chambers of the Heart. 56
Two Jackals. 57
Andre Previn 58
White Reading Helmet. 59
The Animal Passage .60
Freak Inside the Heart 61
Apples on Fire 62
Panda. 63
Sverdlovsk Institute Optimization Theory 64
Water Experiment in Two Parts 65
Otto Frank in Macy's. 66
We Were Almost Home 68
Vision. 69
In the Moment of His Stuck Out Tongue 70
Pinhole 71
Bethe's Tree Experiment 72
The Brothers Stopped Procreating 73

5.

Dune and Swale 76

1.

Opalescent

Your family is in flight. It seems that decades didn't happen or happened all at once. The next few years are all weddings. On the end of holidays we wait for the next holiday. We remember bombed resorts and the constant cigarettes. People danced at parties with no regard for your safety. One summer the playground had long chains with rings and kids broke arms. All those dumb kids are now actors. The hardest thing is to let go of your retinas, to accept that they are dissolving. This terrible gap in your ground, this open maw makes the house less stable. Whether your gem is dusty does not matter. If it is ringed, settling scores, or waiting—all this does not matter. It is natural, no, expected that you are now afraid of everything.

Goose Necks for the Baby Baby

This American pumpkin, father made a cube of it

Drive on a whale bone holding geometry, a physics, and bitted work ethic

Say reconstructed like you mean I never flew at night but my nostrils closed

Bear left at the barber shop and come through

Sit down in an eagle nest while fawns birth a forest

Mrs. Bernstein, my symmetrical head is on that freight train

The Miniature Life of a Raven

Cedar of Lebanon! A raven lives there.
It's okay, complimentary, because he looks
over the highway.

                His family is waiting,
somewhere, occupied in nesting and gleaming
the feather. Somewhere eggs open, crack
in that fragile way.

                A raven on the verge
of his version of the holidays. Did you not think
they celebrated? Sat around pleasantly with jokes?

They have x-rays. Will travel, prevail over something
or everything. One could sit down and question this
particular raven about his uncle, his aunt,
his war hero grandfather.

            He will never make anything more beautiful than
need be, will not use words like cool or glass or platelet.
He is aware of his un-mammothness.

Boy Birds

In the pig barn they found a light. There's a reason things happen. I left home

           and it fell apart. I put salt in some delicate plants and they turned red.
The hacksaw was moving. In that memory always comes a shadow. Some type of menacing farmer.

I keep constructing dioramas. The general store always comes in first. Then the calcified waves. Then the swan's neck hooks water.

Calf's Blood

All I do is drink calf's blood / I've sent up black plates / black pots with stars on the bottom / I burst out, bud the ivy plant and cut diamonds / I walk and scatter chicken feed / I'm not sure if the sea comes close to your city / And are there streets left over / Are the four of us are buried, or perhaps / remaining in some shapes and colors / It's as if we linked arms and closed together / all in agreement that this is no longer our continent / and it is no longer our continent

Technical / Vocational

In the nebulous of pushpins you stand sideways / Look through your eyelids /

The debriefing of Polaroids / Before we leave / Let's find your white gloves /

Go to Europe and model / Your arms are glorious / Your nose a ski slope /

A forced piggy back / I wish a car talked to me / I was a German plenum /

In an old video hair is so so giant / Knees are / Pale and more than beautiful /

More than a third of the kids live below / The poverty / Line / The girls get pregnant /

Is this food authentic? / Is it spicy?? / This depends on a standardized test /

This depends on familial history / Etiquette rules / There is a 67% dropout rate /

This is a lot / We are breaking up large failing schools / Walk down the hall and see /

A dreamer has an attitude / I am somebody

Watch the Village

I know someday I will barbeque and throw my head back. I can see the iron now.

                      I will document my new life as a beaver human.

Below me water pulls itself and nothing makes this everyday,

not even thinking of that cowboy. Sitting here, tiny leaves stuck to face,
I smell thunder,

            at least smell it approaching. The densely packed bushes trap heat,

the branches kaleidoscope the chimneys.

Dangerfields

The brick is placed in fear, as in high school, when fear is evident over dinner. At last, the anesthetic admits fear. I would like another chance at living. I think I could do better. It's about choices. It's turning things over and over in your copper pot. There are secrets to keep from mother. Really, this is for her safety. She once hit a school bus and kept going. She has shotgun panache and you don't know the consequences. They promise G-d is not vengeful, but do they really know that. Look, this isn't about questions, but why do my former doctors hate me. Why are the power lines always close. Outside, the banana leaf tree is enormous, the bamboo invasive, the neighbors severely inbred.

Many Teens Hide Deepest Secrets in Plain Sight

Because there are stars for your teeth, I'm using the gentle hammer to tap out science. The diamond is flawed, deeply grooved with rival glints. The hands move about as if the hammer is joking, as if I'm not serious when knocking the daisy reliquary for our serious eye movement, our pinched nerve ending. When I hold a tomato, light beams through the aisles. How could you know of phantom anything. Maybe I was never ready to say parts moved me, but covered us in leaves. And I believe in the abdomen powers, grazing cattle and meeting in clearings, as if to say I found something whole and feathered, with only the head missing.

Pink and Hot Pink Habitat

They shoot up, the stalks with globular color

orbed with stiff tissue layers poking the air.

You arrange them in water, but do they need water.

The answer is yes. They are alive.

When knocking a vase over, backhand it,

send the globs flying. When visiting college,

you learn that glass is liquid and sloping down.

Backhand your college choices. Arrange an arrangement,

fit into a hounds-tooth jacket. Get a small pipe,

a dried mushroom, and an antique locket.

When people come over, show off your closet.

Your ancient corsets and slovenly coats.

Breasts of America

My father was arrested.

He was selling things in the street.

Cigarettes in a carton. My father.

He told me much later. And I thought

his glasses, did he get to keep them.

Was he also scared to get in a truck

and our math notebook   did he hate it,

are we all arrested and glamorous.

We have two outfits and our legs.

Later we shop for hangers. We are tearing

coming apart, no   we are about to. We are

living for now. Will we save the breasts

of America. No, America will save our breasts.

But they will not look the same! And one is bigger!

Here the dolls have closets, plastic shoes,

and access to the Precambrian.

Düsseldorf is For Sisters

One is Scheherazade, but they both wear overcoats.

One traces rectangles, but they both wear overcoats.

Are you my sister from Mom's uterus? Are you

using a fork in that way? Why does one flower

in our arrangement look so eaten? I'm sailing to you.

I'm sailing to you on white sails. On white cells.

I've recently counted my white cells.

One is a stirrup, but they both ride in saddles.

One has puffy lips, but they both ride in saddles.

I like names like Angela, Angelica, and Stanley.

I like Buford, Blaine, and Tammy. Düsseldorf really

is for sisters. Please bring in the rhinestones,

the leather purses. Bring on the hairpins

and lacquered horses. One wears a metal band,

but they both have pink gums. One doesn't mind

that much, but they both have pink gums.

Autumn. Sugar. Bloodspring.

The leaf of you, the bend, the fire flicker for the Kazak.

        A tree swells and calls on itself,

a mother mothers somewhere behind your knees.

The grass was softest where you left it—

              lit up in the field, in a safe place.

Have you documented? The careful migration,

a predicted wing flap, and what if I was tiny.

School is for the smallest of children, waiting for

the smell of it, maybe returning, maybe arching.

We collect this in sealed jars, and there is a piece of you.

              In a porcelain veneer your tooth cracked,

              bloomed, to signal coming.

It's a twisted sign the way those branches unfolded.

Misarubka

That flock of sheep is puzzle hearts.   I wait after school for safety.

I put cotton in my ears and float to dimension x7y giga heart maggot.

The sweetness factory. Everyone is a flower and human rafts come to shore.

The sleep language is what the eyelids did to each other.

                                                    The stay on x7y giga heart maggot is brief.

The mothers turn icy.   I raft to shore with the ice mothers.

And the earth is not ready. I am here. A bigger version of me above myself. I wait after school for a string of numbers. x7y giga heart maggot is best reached by a river

                   of schools and numbers. Break your arms off. Row to shore. Hallelujah.

2.

Super Dolphin (Super Skin)

Your memory foam leaves it behind.

        The magenta outline of coming to something

        that is not in a cupboard, or the cherry farm,

        or a bird nest.

That does not defecate, and that

could be a miracle. A hidden clue speaks

through wires. Sparks the wing curl,

illuminates the fur feather.

        That stands in rubble, with a fireman, a boot.

        That is a miracle, a holy ghost, a way to powder.

Me in Prison

I suffer and make things worse. Freak myself out. This is me in the prison yard. Help me file down the metal. Last night a voice came from the toilet. I suffer at the makeup counter. The air feels abysmal. What. There is so much disappointment. My friends are in freaky love. Somewhere a hospital is waiting. Somewhere in the future you are waiting. Accidentally I start the time machine. I rattle along and visit dead relatives.

Maybe Someone is Altering Your Throat

In my tangerine themed garden the family reunited.

                                      In parts of Honduras the leaves sweat into one river. Some trees knot together.

These small monkeys have a way of shutting the birds out.

Distant monkeys, distant parental mania.   A nearby coast.

                            There is something chrome in these flowers.

Their penny-blood smell, euphoria, some rage of animals. These bird sanctuaries are covered in invisible netting. Some gold coins are surely in this ruffled ground.

From the Suitcase My Back is an Arrow.

The sky is lit up. I live in Germany with the bluest sky,

I keep that in my sweater. Why is everything melting.

The fish we found in the frozen puddle. You are my pet on a stick.

Oh, waterfalls frozen. At nine o'clock we do arithmetic, and at ten read.

There is no music for months. Put us in that truck.

Give chocolate to the ladies. Racecars to the men. I'm dead right now

and you have the cancer. Can we talk about it. Let's talk about

your cancer. I have two sweaters. One has a house and chimney.

Buffalo Cuffs

      End stop errand boy and the wave that saved him
comparing shoe prices glances lit up, family time the breath of fierceness,

      Telegrams, inkblot, quill change, prints that daughters leave
behind spindle with two legged feet rivered section cake making troops,

      Treeless ravine and petal marks, hesitant beast, hairlocked chin star breaking the sidewalk, teacher born, teacher pointed, teacher dancer,

      Huff committee, diamond crane and sink, gem drain diamond whisper, nailed saddle, coma of your favorite spot, electric paddle and thrust strokes. They hear you still, voice box annie, the winter's horse ride.

Weakened Astronauts

We synchronized our ways and traveled by wagons.

The picture came into view. A wave overtaking ships.

The rust grew more orange. We never recover from this.

Wingspans' quiet. Point Pleasant. Mount. Carmel. Flatbush.

Succulent tribes dot the horizon. Rhubarb in strips.

Star fruit. Some people drive it and keep going.

Western ho. Unrolling scripts in front of you. Land ho.

Deprivation chambers. Flight Simulators. Horse drawn carriages.

The first person to speak. Orbiting for the first time.

New Jersey Seems Magical

Strawberries, horses, and bows become buttons. Become miniature Americana with traditional breakfast. We stumbled on a fairground, there was a chained monkey. On another continent a chained bear. Spinning around fast, approaching something like a hypnotic nausea, the dance of the seven veils reminded us of delicious meat. Just when I realized how much of a girl I was I realized how much of a boy I was. Awkward with my big hands fumbling for the big buttons on her yellow sweater. She held me off with a gilded fork. Approaching something like the biggest ball of yarn we took pictures. We could have made a wrong turn anywhere. When driving it is always possible never to come back by moving to a new town with a new identity.
I never told you about that camp in North Carolina. I dabbed blood on my cheek. I wanted to die there.

No One is Brunswick Turbulon

Wood Splinter.   Accordion Jumper.

A mother holds someone and says Cranberry Pain.

Will you marry me, Five Magnet?

Today is Halloween and we dress it.

Clamp Mudface is a gangster. Jobs Treading is fluttering wheat.

Even the temperature is white in winter, says Staircase Redstone.

Tower Babelash smiles and runs up it. Gasoline Crank rolls forward.

Somewhere in Ohio Jester McBroomsticks follows the wrong person home.

Straw Water and Homo Hope sit together in class.

They whisper to Horse Abdomen. Hold hands in gym class.

Miss Sarajevo

Wears her own crown. By the entrance, flowers.
An idea of learned helplessness. Such as, when a
child does not know where to find a new glue stick.
Such as a pageant, where lucite strikes the faux-
cobble stone. Diagrams reveal an overlap of interests:
tennis and high fashion. Tennis because of hyper
balls, and high fashion because of cruelty in
the swagger. Miss Sarajevo walking across the stage,
by the entrance, flowers. A sense of removal from
that which is violent. From that which keeps
entering itself into the pageant. A unicorn is a mythical
being, much like Miss Sarajevo, walking somehow
straight and not at all violent.

Mathematic Horse

What to say when we found her. Ice capped. Hair bound. In the eye a hint of grandma a memory of chicken coop and the heart. There is earth and ice and earth and island. There are paper etchings and brain function. There is brain function at various temperatures. Brain function in memory. In memory there are two islands. Two chicken coops. Two hearts. Always a measure of rib expansion for the extreme racing of the heart. There is always a measure of your father and his wingspan. The polar caps hold quiet. The hands that hold sleep. The egg of horses and migration. There once was a migration. What to say when we found her. Ice capped. Hair bound.

The Cloisters

Demented island, whitish hot air balloons,

hundreds of them landing with no trouble,

tender boats and waiting. I'm traveling with

people. It's a dog in that window, and it's waiting.

The electric gems show their horseness,

their speed ability. I'm traveling this

in the Queen's English, and His Holiness

the 14th Dali Lama makes me better. I'm

staying out later due to a glimmer infection.

I'm pulsing stars in my abdomen, a slow trickle

of them leaking out. The bells ring out

and there is a promise of cake. I'm designing

houses with my brother architect.

Great Sophias

There were two great Sophias
and a few good Dorothys. We enacted
inside the outside world of the mausoleum.

The mausoleum is by my house,
and I thought it was ordinary. I thought
it was all ordinary. I was Sophia,
but not so good at it. I loved Dorothy.

On the lake, the small swans stood on water.
I stood under a tree. Someone occupied the
peace pagoda. It is not always certain,
a safe exit from the forest.

I believe their show was the first
to address homosexuality. Dorothy
loved the way she dressed.
They were dressed impeccably.

The Decorating Committee

They carried knives that day and a theme was chosen. The science club, their thermometers. There is a theory that they knew what was knocking. There is a theory that Robert, who sustained the first touch, saw the microscope tremble.

Imagine the double doors and Robert.

There are a million and one uses for the glass beaker case. Look at the way it bisects Susan. Dr. Putnam, your tie has never looked more appropriate, peaking out through your heaving back. Thank you for showing them the universe.

(Dr. Putnam sat in his office.

The science club was working on a new theory.

It stated that the atom was actually

a fragment of time, most likely two weeks ago,

crystallized, detached, and floating.)

A) Geography

A) sand dispute. A) bus divergence. A) zebra run.

B) The cannon party back porched. B) The way your skewer smells.

*A) landlocked continent. *A) river in a time of rivers.

"The flight was lovely." "Only a piece of me is missing."

A) bunker. A) way to harvest. A) small force still brick travels.

B) The way a belly looks. B) The essential rice. B) The journey to the middle.

A) glacial need. A) shift in continents. A) crank to push it.

B) The scatter line for other lines. B) The something strands.

*A) rush to cockpit. A) field study. *A) way to spiral.

Jeffrey Bloodhound Sans

I know him. To know is dimension,
a black bot with star spangles. Have
a sexy birthday. Have an amalgamation.
The language was just delivered and it
is good.
                    I'm holding secret.
                    This situation. Countdown. Speeches for
                    if I don't come back. I'm not coming back.

In profile with gold necklace. The quiet ears. Study the
nose. Today I become naked Ingrid. Would Ingrid
mind a morsel of finger fat.

Girl words. A tomato. A plum. An apricot.
                    Time is holding in a clear tube.
                    Time is lightning on a spare key.

Words that do not yet exist. Alibubo. Bubsigtree. Grivstalbikt.

3.

All Night Vigil

The idea of ancient dust on velvet
somehow brings together a missile crisis,
a place that holds keys to falling forward.
Move closer to a city, to a bakery,
point a rifle skyward. Some skin shines
under a disco light, friends leave the city in pairs,
holding hands and tucking their furs under
blankets. My father pirouettes stage right,
the blue light bounces off his white tights.
All night vigil for Dijermo and Durango,
where I'm told no one dresses well.
I hold another vigil for all the times
I made grandma wrestle us to the ground.

All night vigil is to fly a plane on a holy holiday.
All night vigil for always rebuilding.
I ask forgiveness for not keeping an all night vigil
when the bombs keep a greenish vigil of their own.
I keep an all night vigil for my father's choices,
for his strangeness and tank-ability.

When a light comes on, hands are visible.
If it's an intruder, yell very loudly
and I'll answer. I'll call the police with
the red and blue lights. If only your body is left,
I promise a certain relief, as an officer lifts
a small section of hair off of your open mouth.
I promise an all night candle vigil for your body.
I promise to put my yearly reflections
in small columns.

All night vigil for not returning
to that continent. All night vigil for
a church that turned into a gymnasium,
complete with swimming pool.
I keep an all night vigil for the Kunstkammer,
which keeps an all night vigil
for the deformed skeletons it houses,
and I keep an all night vigil for them too.

Another vigil for my drunken neighbor,
as she hollered government conspiracy.
She put her leg onto train tracks.
She swung her arms as her phantom
infants baked bread. All night vigil
for phantoms and baking.

All night vigil for Mrs. Emily Bossin
and spelling tests, green sweaters and parts
of New Jersey, Boston, and Atlanta.
Keep a vigil for all doctors,
what they don't know.
Taking bits of pink nose bone out
of nostrils. With a tiny headlight
they see inside, but only so far.
No, don't tell me about that day or
paper flying. All night vigil for disabling
news service and all updates. I'm going
to carve something in a piece of leather
for a son to find.

When shining a light on
dry milk, a text is visible. A sheath with
binding keeps the letters straight, secret
in a breast pocket. All night vigil for old
documents strapping parts of one family
to another. All night vigil for dead world
leaders. With this idea I sculpt a new
nose with my gentle hammer. Here,
the skin pulls tighter and the boats
take off toward the square horizon.

All night vigil is to roller skate.
To hold hours in a circle.
A little heat is extinguished by the rug,
and the books press whatever it is
into your hands. Documents,
documents of a country years ago.
Photos of graying people.
To roller-skate without falling
is to complete a circle under spinny lights,
to photograph a rupture in the netting.

4.

Von Furstenberg

The milk was slightly pink.

                A hole formed over father.

This medicine makes foam at the mouth. At the end of the world I left by train. The phones didn't work.

        This vortex opened in the sky. Then there were fireballs.

There Are Four Chambers of the Heart

There are four chambers of the heart, but only one holds a bent toothpick. One keeps the careful excavation of a mammoth and tusks
the pants I constructed   a leftover bruise. Between the four of them, there are two secrets, and three ways for saying leafy webbings. The third chamber is the keeper of light and old school uniforms, also my apron and a busted lip. The fourth chamber is for unrepeatable things father said   a camel with three bullet holes   a crushed pewter ball   a dead rabbit I sent someone to find.

There were three things I sent my father to find. Appendicitis and a brief hospital stay. The dead rabbit. It only reached the lawn after he placed it there. It was too light for my fingers, but with him it took on an unnatural weight.

There were two excavated mammoth tusks. Inside the mouth they found a pewter ball and a camel with three bullet holes. Also sand, and a delicate wrist watch. The mammoth froze with her front right leg raised. The cold moved so quickly then.

There is one thing my father said. I could hear it because he said it so loudly. I thought of the immigration officers. I wanted to tell them, we do not need a country. We can destroy ourselves here.

Two Jackals

The jackal dressed me in the storefront,
a jacket and wide belt and lace-up shoes.

To a customer nearby I mouthed "Don't
leave me." The jackal's sinister intentions,
she did not want me to speak.

                                        Fine, I said.
Give me the jacket.

                      And now the room is dark.
The exit blocked by wooden carts. I yell upstairs.
The jackal is behind me.

                              A second jackal
descends a staircase, and raises her arms,
aims them out into her crazed sister. They retreat,
pointing whole hands at each other.

Andre Previn

Sharon loves everything about my new penis.

    I built something glassy for the catacombs.

        I brushed honey out of some deep mouth caves. Under New York are the albino rat and alligator. Under Paris there is a painting of a mist. A bride's cataract eye.

Dick super ruby. There aren't enough carves in this prospect. Shield the cornea from direct sunlight. Your genes are destined to do this anyway.

White Reading Helmet

He held the animals to him (the wintered kind).

     Some girls were really gigantic. Some detached into the atmosphere.

He held the ceremonial sheet of water. The accident finally happened

and now the consequence. We all lost something in that tall grass. Father was an unruly meadow, an unyielding mushroom cloud. See, at first it all seemed unbelievable. We started hating the children. Their needs were insufficient.

See, he found some loophole in the grammar. He held that flapping fish and fondly. Some heat came from our mouths and we smuggled things. And next time I ask for smoked meat I hope you bring it. Ride on into it. The heat of my left nostril.

The Animal Passage

The antelope braided shotgun, the antelope braided with a shotgun,

a possibility of children flying past the truck tops. Interstate blaring

for the antelope leading a parade, she moves the pots and chops

the vegetables. Across the street a child goes missing,

a cheekbone is implanted. Is the mother mad when she finds the child.

He is pearl scattered in the grass, combed and glistening.

Freak Inside the Heart

There were exquisite surgeons under lamplight,

there was a breeze before surgery.

Before surgery the doctors took notes.

I refused to speak with Satan, there

was really no need for that contact. The mound

was small, there were so many other cities,

three hundred years ago bells still rang, and now

a broken steam pipe by the cemetery. I said,

the city is a comfort. I said, check the fire exit.

I said, clear away the thicket of berries, the

mess hall rang with spoons, the clocks pointed

to the end of talking, there was really nothing

left to say. There was a sort of honesty in our

killing. It made the rest sit together. It made

the news deliver messages. It made history make

room for us. It bought flowers in lieu of flowers.

Then they reconsidered knitting. Reconsidered not

offering rides home. They took out the kaleidoscopes

and gemstones. They made one giant kaleidoscope

and felt like gentlemen. Like gentle men.

Apples on Fire

My father spoke to me but did not see me. When we spoke he was watery and I was solid. In the past I planned our future. We could not meet in restaurants. In the past he was a stag and I was a reindeer, but in the future he was thunderous and I was misty. When planning our future together I said "You have to hear me" and he said
"Feel this here pain" I said "This house was in the underground railroad" and he said "Whatever happened at prom?"

At prom I was crispy and my date was cusped.

We are both horned animals but we are worlds apart.

Panda

Why don't you fuck, panda? Why don't you birth something?
Instead you eat your way to extinction. Your punch black eyes.
Panda. Your temper like the frontal lobe. Shattered but clicking.
We love your fatness. Every fat fucking part of you. We can wait for you.

For your panda fucking. For your throbbing paws. Make us a promise, panda.

Make a panda, panda. Make it slow giant. We import you. Look at you.

You sit on your glorious asses. You lick each other. We need your panda sex.

We need your thumbprints to save this process.

Sverdlovsk Institute Optimization Theory

Construction work and chocolate butter, maybe some sweater modeling,
or a kitten of some sorts, and the place rings so loud at night,

    and everyone is   happy to be there and you like it,

and you want to buy some candy, and you put on all of your jewelry at once and wear a revealing shirt and roller skates, and no one thinks you are cool, and the neighbor talks about G-d, and you like it, and you like all the colors and pretending to be good at sports, and your neighbor invites you over to sing about portable hand grenades, and your dad wears a giant top hat and your grandma wears a Choctaw headdress, and it's crazy but it really happened, and

it felt like something sat down and died, but you found it had a treasure in its pocket, and you took it because that's what it wanted, and then the music came on and you felt good about yourself, and the world, and your teeth were crooked, and your nose was getting ready, and you had no idea that you were something, that something mattered, and that it was all happening and it was so beautiful that it could have rained in a slow motion but you remember your first desk, it was December, and the wood was cold but you sat in it anyway, and later someone fat would jump on you, and it was pain like something, and you wanted to talk about it in a cup   made for crying in America.

Water Experiment in Two Parts

I.

A scientific study reveals: water is alive.

Equal amounts of water is poured into three identical containers.

Zelig Berken died fighting in world war II.

Equal amounts of rice is poured into each container.

Zelig Berken was twenty years old.

The first container is told "I hate you." The second container is told "I don't care about you." and the third container is told "I love you very much."

While Zelig Berken was away at war his entire town was evacuated.

The rice in the first container turned black. The rice in the second container bloomed. And the rice in the third container rotted.

II.

Water is poured into two identical containers.

The first container goes home with Scientist A.

The second goes to church with Scientist B.

The next day, a droplet is extracted from each container.

The droplet from the first container shows nothing of significance.

The droplet from the second container shows formations of stars

and giant flowers.

Otto Frank in Macy's

Arranging the shoe horns, walking
with customers, being very young
and unaware, here we follow Otto
as he dusts the glove counter, fixes a
broken light bulb. Look out, Otto, that
jacket is on the floor, that hanger is
faulty. Otto, clever foreign Otto,
lovely languid Otto. Naked river
Otto, fire building Otto, far from quiet
Otto, so complicated and not seeing
that much into the future. Not pursuing
the future, no, not really looking into it.
Otto on the spinning teacups,
on a wooden rollercoaster, eating lobster
(Otto in a big lobster bib), laughing Otto,
drunk and angry Otto, at the Nutcracker,
front row with a handful of white flowers,
picking mushrooms, Otto bent over in the forest,
with a straw basket and wide hat, Otto
driving a Ford, changing a tire, telephoning
all of Europe, Otto's rhetoric, his ideas on
war politics, Otto in profile, in argument,
riding a horse, carefully, at the dentist and
then buying some stamps, Otto existing in
a bookstore, waiting for his taxi, there's Otto
in a hammock, reading about native species,
filling out documents, at the Chrysler building,
at the airport, with a newspaper and clean socks,
Otto, somehow not realizing, on a wooden
rollercoaster, screaming, trying a cartwheel,
eating hot dogs, somehow not realizing, Otto,

at conception, before heartbeat, being human
Otto, flying, Otto at ten in the bathtub,
at fifteen, a head-on portrait, at twenty learning
in a tight jacket, growing and being amazing.
Otto of the future in all silver floating
with satellites over everything, over colors.

We Were Almost Home

Though we did not see the Artillery Museum

the river erupted into circular fountains.

We were both called good boys

and worked on our handwriting.

So what, I said, so the museum is lost?

We sat in silence and thought zoology.

The key here was the Mammoth.

Seeing it was opera and ice skating.

I've always thought stretching canvases

sounds important. And here it was.

We left a green cannon partially exposed.

Vision

The world was not yet discovered.
             It traveled in a galaxy of dinosaur bones and other fossils.

Embedded and waiting. Waiting for decades

when the skirts were different.

When Mr. O watered his plants in a light blue shirt with a breast pocket. His hair slicked back, he boarded a plane to Africa, where the lion still walked in bursts of grass.

In his light blue rental car, Mr. O took photos, very close photos, of lions resting.

There was nothing to report back.

The world lay silent. The giant squid was silent.
The continents were silent. It was quiet as he boarded the plane for home.

It was quiet in the diamond mines, it was quiet in the coal mines,

And the Loch Ness monster sighed and waited for sonar.

In the Moment of His Stuck Out Tongue

In the moment of his stuck out tongue we discovered loneliness.

Discovered how a sweater covers the body. A ball skipped a turn
and here are octopi in warm waters.

There, we floated backwards on a golden river. Even the canes were polished
and the day was a holiday.

Every small hotel owner closed his eyes.

The fabric fed through machines with forever mechanisms chomping.

Pinhole

A yellowish liquid slid off a fang hanging
slender necked, the lady was trumpeting,
holding court. You have made a cuckold
of me. Stamp collecting and small photographs
both organized yet not in a natural order.
I wanted to ask about that night or that time
your ring slipped. Pipes taken apart still
hid the articles inside themselves, as quiet
gangsters or stenographers. Is there a word
for climbing a stair in a most mysterious way.
To cut up a magazine and paste together ransom
notes, magnanimous. To place a squirrel behind
a partition of almond glass an almost holy rite.
You came this way, a stopwatch and
sweatband included, hiding geometry in the
left armpit and holding a dirty photograph.
My squid is just so deep down right now.
No spear or boy in fringed bottoms can swim
that straight.

Bethe's Tree Experiment

We go in circles. We are on a slight tilt.
Point A. Point A is Selma. There had been
previous attempts on Selma. Then, symbolic
marches. Later, an attempt to return butterflies
to the gardens. Bethe claimed that bees
are the after moment. After something, a
swarm of them. To gently send bees into
a fog is a calming influence. Point B is
the early life and founding of a temple.
Point B deals with Wings of Deliverance.
The People's Temple. And revolutionary
suicide. Bees are widely known to self destruct.
They are often followers of a bigger force.
Bethe, who previously claimed that bees are
the after moment failed to report his time
travel experiment. The circle is stacked so that
Point T rests under Point B. Point T is the
Lodz Ghetto. The last liquidated. The most
productive. A goldmine with workshops.
Bethe claimed that survival depends on work
ethic. The bee is entirely dependent on
outside sources. There was no resistance in
the Lodz ghetto. Compare this with Warsaw,
Vilna, and Bialystock. Bethe claimed symbolic,
polemic, and defensive resistance and
sometimes sabotage are the bee weapons.
These bring about a certain hive order,
a killing machine of sorts.

The Brothers Stopped Procreating

It was a new day on earth. I was dumb.

Someone took buttons to my ribs. Blue

and yellow ones. Then we stopped for

cabbage. I've always feared animal attacks.

I don't like the beady eyed animals. Their

tongues are fiery. This fancy candle

burns in a study. Up north, they eat turnips.

They are not so worried there. I'm worried

here. I like the idea of power. Like grandfather

crushing chocolate with his finger.

5.

Dune and Swale

I'm thinking of my teeth right now and the white sparks they give off as they glint in the sunlight of my jaw. I'm thinking of the chariot race and white rabbits. I'm thinking of an ocean, of a hurricane, of a boat ride, of an assassin, of a field, of a snow drift, of a forest, and of my skin as it rests here in the star throne. Fields, places of beginning, and, as I'm sure you know, there was a beginning for all of us. Last night I held a rabbit and his breathing and his heart. I had a strong desire to turn him into a constellation and flower seed at the same time.

Towns, is it possible that words are brick heavy and connecting. Is it possible to feel three heartbeats at the same time. Last night I thought of an ocean and of a field, one on top of the other and then back again. Everything goes here and if you stand with me long enough I will show you the underside and the belly of my fastest horse. You have not seen green as I have. There is no grace left here and you will not mourn it. To put it more plainly, there is no grace in a wing of any kind. There is nothing left but horses and their fields of violet. You have not seen violet as I have.

Dark and stationary, the still of you and the shift of our continent. Love is an equine. Love is a parachute and you are in it. Have you seen my knife? Have you seen the woods behind your house? The way your vein pulsated tells me you are thinking. The way your vein pulsated is decadent. It is a slow climb to your mountain.

Equine thoughts and butterfly preservation. I wonder for the binding of paper, the way it lets us bisect the moment of grace, which still does not exist. You are the smallest leaf, the clearest webbing, and you hold the birds, all their noise to your clavicle.

Humans are G-d's secret architecture and your mother is the cupola of maple leaves. I have put myself here, in this orb of muscle and wonderment, grain, gold, silk, and the map of roads. I have been here before, bent sideways in water, bent sideways in a field of grain, and I no longer wish for that.

There are no identical breaths out of your distant mouth. I have put my hands on it, on the beating heart of your absence, and the decision has been made. All that bleeds does so in search of better versions.

I remember. There is a body and his mouth was attached. There is no economy like the beauty of his hands. There are diamonds and roads and ways of sleeping. I wonder about your carving nature and the lumber you vanished.

I wonder about the pears you left out. I wonder if your shoulders move as the earth makes room for your body. I no longer question the logic of migration, but I also refuse to open my lips farther than one centimeter.

I'm thinking of the kinetic equation that might get us there, at the foot of the Lord, into the valley of powder horses. I broke a small part of myself. I broke what lay inside and constructed a shallow pool for our gazelles and antelopes.

There is a rift deep inside my nest of organs and it is building itself a second rift so that I may fall into it. My voice is constructed of dings in the crystal goblet and it carries over the ocean into your porcelain ear. I unfold and settle into myself.

I can be still here, in the hollow of the space a different heart left behind. I call out a name. Language comes in prisms and I cradle it as an animal mother. Grant me the silence and the unmoving birth of our contact.

There is weight not only in water but also in my limbs as they submerge then resurface. And I still refuse the grace of your being. The ripening movement of that grace shifted my ribcage and altered the sated gram.

Acknowledgements

The author wishes to thank the following publications in which some poems from this book first appeared: Best New Poets 2007, Coconut, Invisible Ear, Model Homes, Octopus, Skein, Soft Blow, Unpleasant Events Schedule, Verse.com, and Weird Deer. Additional thanks to Factory Hollow Press for including works by the author in the chapbooks Poems For Lidija and The Conduct of Bees in the Buckwheat Season. Finally, a thank you to Seth Landman for editing a chapbook titled American Chemistry in which a selection of the poems in this book first appeared together.

Great thanks to: Brian Henry, Peter Gizzi, and Dara Wier.

Much gratitude and appreciation to: Bruce Covey, Shanna Compton, Matt Cipov and Jon Link.

The author has a lot of love for her family and friends in Atlanta, Athens, Boston, Charlottesville, Detroit, Northampton, New York City, Philadelphia, Reston, and Tel Aviv and is grateful for their enthusiasm and support.

www.ingramcontent.com/pod-product-compliance
Lightning Source LLC
Chambersburg PA
CBHW031207090426
42736CB00009B/814